SHEO: A Guide to Female Entrepreneurship and Financial Freedom

Ashona Fyffe

Abpersonnelservices.com/legaldocumentpreparation

Copyright © 2024 Ashona Fyffe

All rights reserved. No part of this book may be reproduced, distributed, or transmitted in any form or by any means, including photocopying, recording, or other electronic or mechanical methods, without the prior written permission of the publisher, except in the case of brief quotations embodied in critical reviews and certain other noncommercial uses permitted by copyright law.

For permission requests, write to the publisher at the address below:

A& B Personnel Services LLC

1204 Village Market PL

Suite 306

Morrisville, NC 27560

assistant@abpersonnelservices.com

abpersonnelservices.com/legaldocumentpreparation

This book is provided for informational purposes only. The author and publisher make no representations or warranties with respect to the accuracy or completeness of the contents of this book and specifically disclaim any implied warranties of merchantability or fitness for a particular purpose. The advice and strategies contained herein may not be suitable for every situation. The author and publisher shall not be liable for any loss of profit or any other commercial damages, including but not limited to special, incidental, consequential, or other damages.

Trademarked names, logos, and images appearing in this book are the property of their respective owners and are used for identification purposes only. Their inclusion does not imply any endorsement or affiliation with the book.

Cover design by Queen Calico

Book design by Ashona Fyffe

Printed in United States

First Edition: April, 2024

To my amazing children, mommy loves you!

To the strong and inspiring women in my life, including my mother, sisters, aunts, cousins, close friends, mentors, and colleagues. Your unwavering support and encouragement have fueled my journey as an entrepreneur, and I am grateful for your love and inspiration.

To the resilient spirit and boundless potential of women worldwide. May we shatter barriers, defy expectations, and forge a future where every woman can thrive and rise to her fullest potential.

"The most effective way to do it, is to do it."– *Amelia Earheart*

Table of Contents

Introduction: The Power of Female Entrepreneurship

Chapter 1: Unleashing Female Entrepreneurship: Why it Matters

- Why Female Entrepreneurship Matters

- The Power of Women in Business

- Overcoming Barriers and Challenges

Chapter 2: Finding Your Passion and Purpose

- Discovering Your Strengths and Skills

- Identifying Your Niche Market

- Turning Your Passion into Profit

Chapter 3: 20 Lucrative Business Ideas for Female Entrepreneurs

Chapter 4: Building a Solid Foundation

- Setting Clear Goals and Objectives
- Creating a Business Plan
- Legal Considerations for Entrepreneurs
- Importance of Good Bookkeeping

Chapter 5: The Power of Mindset and Confidence

- Overcoming Self-Doubt and Imposter Syndrome
- Cultivating a Positive Mindset
- Building Confidence in Yourself and Your Business

Chapter 6: Strategic Branding and Marketing

- Crafting Your Brand Identity
- Developing a Marketing Strategy
- Utilizing Social Media and Online Platforms

Chapter 7: Financial Management and Wealth Building

- Budgeting and Financial Planning

- Managing Cash Flow and Expenses

- Investing for Long-Term Success

Chapter 8: Scaling Your Business for Six Figures

- Scaling Strategies and Growth Opportunities

- Leveraging Technology and Automation

- Building a Strong Team and Network

Chapter 9: Overcoming Obstacles and Resilience

- Dealing with Setbacks and Failures

- Overcoming Fear of Failure

- Building Resilience and Perseverance

Chapter 10: Nurturing Work-Life Harmony

- Prioritizing Self-Care and Wellbeing

- Achieving Work-Life Balance

- Managing Family and Business Responsibilities

Chapter 11: Paying It Forward: Empowering Other Women

- Mentorship and Support Networks

- Giving Back to the Community

- Being a Catalyst for Change

Conclusion

Introduction: The Power of Female Entrepreneurship

Female entrepreneurship is not just about making money; it's about creating opportunities, breaking barriers, and empowering women to realize their full potential. In today's world, women are still underrepresented in many industries, facing discrimination, and systemic barriers that hinder their progress. However, entrepreneurship offers a pathway to financial freedom, independence, and empowerment for women from all walks of life. This book is a testament to the power of female entrepreneurship and a guide to help women make six figures starting from scratch. It's a beacon of hope for women seeking a way out of domestic violence situations, toxic work environments, or the guilt of balancing career and family responsibilities. Through the chapters that follow, I hope to inspire and empower women to take control of their destinies, build successful businesses, and create a better future for themselves and their communities. SHEO is your roadmap to success in the world of female entrepreneurship. Let's embark on this journey together and unleash the potential of female entrepreneurship.

Chapter 1: Unleashing Female Entrepreneurship: Why it Matters

Female entrepreneurship is a movement that empowers women to realize their full potential and contribute to economic growth and social change. In this chapter, we'll explore the significance of female entrepreneurship, the transformative power of women in business, and the keys to unlocking success in the entrepreneurial journey. Through inspiring examples and actionable insights, we'll delve into how female entrepreneurship can be a force for innovation, inclusivity, and empowerment in today's world.

Why Female Entrepreneurship Matters

The Female Entrepreneurship movement is reshaping the business landscape and driving economic growth worldwide. Women-owned businesses are on the rise, with women starting businesses at a rate faster than ever before. But why does female entrepreneurship matter? It matters because it creates opportunities, asserts transformation, and empowers women to achieve their full potential.

When women succeed in business, everyone benefits. Women entrepreneurs contribute to job creation, economic development, and community empowerment. They bring fresh perspectives, unique insights, and diverse talents to the table, driving innovation and fueling growth in industries across the board. By harnessing the power of female entrepreneurship, we can unlock new opportunities, drive progress, and build a more inclusive and equitable economy for all.

The Power of Women in Business

Women have always been natural-born leaders, innovators, and problem-solvers. From running households to leading organizations, women have a unique ability to multitask, adapt to change, and navigate challenges with resilience and grace. Yet, for too long, women have been sidelined, underestimated, and overlooked in the business world.

But times are changing. Today, women are breaking barriers, shattering glass ceilings, and redefining success on their own terms. Women-owned businesses are thriving in diverse industries, from technology and finance to healthcare and fashion. Women entrepreneurs are not just building successful businesses; they are also championing causes, driving social change, and inspiring the next generation of leaders.

The power of women in business lies in their ability to lead with empathy, collaborate with others, and create environments where everyone can thrive. This creates the effect that makes a difference in the world.

Overcoming Barriers and Challenges

Despite the progress we've made, women still face significant barriers and challenges in the world of entrepreneurship. From gender bias and discrimination to lack of access to capital and resources, women entrepreneurs often encounter obstacles that their male counterparts do not. These barriers can hinder their ability to start and grow their businesses, limiting their potential and stifling their success.

But women are resilient. They are natural problem-solvers and masters of adaptation. Women entrepreneurs have learned to navigate these barriers with creativity, determination, and perseverance. They have forged their own paths, built their own networks, and overcome obstacles that once seemed insurmountable.

Moreover, as more women break into entrepreneurship, they are paving the way for others to follow. They are creating networks of support, mentorship, and empowerment that lift others up and break down barriers for future generations. Through collective action and collaboration, women entrepreneurs are dismantling the systemic barriers that have held them back and creating a more level playing field for all.

The Gender Gap in Entrepreneurship

Despite the significant strides made by women in entrepreneurship, a gender gap still persists. Women-owned businesses tend to be smaller, grow at a slower pace, and face greater challenges accessing capital and resources compared to their male-owned counterparts. This disparity not only limits the economic potential of women but also hinders overall economic growth and innovation.

One of the key factors contributing to the gender gap in entrepreneurship is access to capital. Women entrepreneurs often struggle to secure funding for their businesses, facing bias and discrimination from investors and financial institutions. This lack of access to capital can hinder their ability to start and grow their businesses, limiting their potential for success.

Moreover, women entrepreneurs also face barriers in accessing networks, mentorship, and support systems. The lack of representation and visibility of women in leadership roles can make it difficult for aspiring female entrepreneurs to find role models and mentors who can guide them on their entrepreneurial journey.

Addressing the Gender Gap

Addressing the gender gap in entrepreneurship requires a multi-faceted approach that tackles systemic barriers and promotes gender equality in all aspects of the business ecosystem. This includes:

1. Increasing Access to Capital: Financial institutions and investors must address gender bias and discrimination in funding decisions and provide equal access to capital for women entrepreneurs.

2. Promoting Diversity and Inclusion: Companies and organizations must prioritize diversity and inclusion in their hiring, procurement, and leadership practices to create more opportunities for women-owned businesses.

3. Providing Mentorship and Support: Establishing mentorship programs, quality education and training, networking events, and support systems tailored to women

entrepreneurs can help provide them with the guidance, resources, and connections they need to succeed.

4. Advocating for Policy Change: Policymakers must enact policies that support women entrepreneurs, such as providing tax incentives, access to affordable childcare, and eliminating gender bias in government procurement and contracting.

Herstory of Powerful Women in Business

Throughout history, women have demonstrated their resilience, creativity, and leadership as entrepreneurs. From Madam C.J. Walker, the first female self-made millionaire in America, to Mary Kay Ash, the founder of Mary Kay Cosmetics, women have overcome the barriers set to prevent access to advancement and exceeded expectations in the business world. Here are a few examples of influential female entrepreneurs:

1. Madam C.J. Walker: Born Sarah Breedlove, Madam C.J. Walker overcame poverty and discrimination to build a beauty empire. She revolutionized the haircare industry for African American women and became one of the wealthiest self-made women of her time.

2. Mary Kay Ash: Mary Kay Ash founded Mary Kay Cosmetics with the mission of empowering women to achieve financial success. Her company became a global powerhouse, offering women the opportunity to build their own businesses and pursue their dreams.

3. Kalpana Saroj: Kalpana Saroj rose from a difficult childhood in India to become a successful businesswoman and philanthropist. She overcame adversity and social barriers to establish herself as a leader in the real estate and manufacturing industries.

4. Janice Bryant Howroyd: Janice Bryant Howroyd is the founder and CEO of ActOne Group, one of the largest privately-held staffing

firms in the world. As an African American woman, she has broken barriers in the business world and championed diversity and inclusion.

5. Rebecca Alvarez: Rebecca Alvarez is the founder of Bloomi, a pioneering sexual wellness platform. Born and raised in a vibrant Hispanic community, Alvarez recognized the need for inclusive, safe, and high-quality intimate care products. With a passion for empowering women and a commitment to destigmatizing conversations around sexual health, she embarked on a mission to create Bloomi.

6. Alice Chang: Alice Chang is the visionary founder of Perfect Corp, a groundbreaking beauty tech company revolutionizing the way consumers experience makeup and skincare. With a background in computer science and a passion for beauty, Chang combined her expertise to create innovative augmented reality beauty apps like YouCam Makeup and Skin Diary. Perfect Corp became the first Taiwan-based software on the New York Stock Exchange.

Conclusion

Female entrepreneurship is a force for change, empowerment, and economic growth. By supporting women entrepreneurs, we can create a more inclusive and equitable world where every woman can succeed. Throughout this book, we will explore the tools, strategies, and mindset shifts needed to make six figures starting from scratch. Together, let's unleash the power of female entrepreneurship and build a brighter future for women everywhere.

Inspirational Quotes

"To any woman who has ever doubted her power, remember: you are capable of achieving greatness beyond your wildest dreams." - Unknown

"Entrepreneurship is not just about making money; it's about making a difference and leaving a legacy that inspires others to follow in your footsteps." - Oprah Winfrey

"Success is not about the destination; it's about the journey and the lessons learned along the way. Embrace the challenges, celebrate the victories, and never lose sight of your vision." - Serena Williams

"Behind every successful woman is herself. Believe in your abilities, trust your instincts, and never let anyone dim your light." - Michelle Obama

Chapter 2: Uncovering Your Passion and Purpose

Embarking on the journey of entrepreneurship begins with understanding your passion, purpose, and unique strengths. In this chapter, we'll explore how to identify your passions, leverage your skills, find your niche market, and transform your passions into a profitable business venture.

1. Discovering Your Passions and Strengths

Start by reflecting on your interests, hobbies, and activities that bring you joy and fulfillment. Consider your natural talents, skills, and strengths, both professionally and personally. Ask yourself what tasks or projects you excel at and what energizes you.

2. Identifying Your Niche Market

Once you've identified your passions and strengths, research potential niche markets that align with your interests and expertise. Look for underserved or untapped market segments where you can provide unique value or solve specific problems. Consider factors such as market demand, competition, and target audience demographics.

3. Turning Your Passion into Profit

Next, explore how you can monetize your passion by offering products or services that cater to your niche market's needs and preferences. Brainstorm business ideas and revenue streams that leverage your skills and align with your passions. Whether it's launching an online store, providing consulting services, or teaching workshops, find a business model that allows you to turn your passion into profit.

4. Building Your Brand and Market Presence

Develop a compelling brand identity that communicates your values, expertise, and unique selling proposition to your target audience. Invest in building a professional online presence through a website, social media profiles, and content marketing efforts. Establish yourself as an authority in your niche by sharing valuable content, engaging with your audience, and showcasing your expertise.

5. Setting Goals and Taking Action

Finally, set clear goals and action plans to bring your business idea to life. Break down your goals into actionable steps, set deadlines, and hold yourself accountable for progress. Stay flexible and open to feedback, adapting your strategies as needed to navigate challenges and seize opportunities along the way.

By uncovering your passion and purpose, identifying your strengths and skills, finding your niche market, and turning your passion into profit, you can embark on a fulfilling entrepreneurial journey that aligns with your values, interests, and goals. With dedication, perseverance, and a willingness to take calculated risks, you can build a successful business that not only generates income but also makes a positive impact on the lives of others.

Chapter 3: Top 20 Business Ideas for Female Entrepreneurs

Aspiring female entrepreneurs often face the challenge of finding business ideas that are not only profitable but also require minimal startup capital. In this chapter, we'll explore 20 lucrative business ideas that have the potential to generate six figures for female entrepreneurs with little to no startup money.

1. Virtual Assistant Services: Offer administrative, clerical, and technical support services to busy professionals and entrepreneurs remotely.

2. Freelance Writing and Editing: Utilize your writing skills to provide content creation, editing, and proofreading services to businesses, bloggers, and publishers.

3. Social Media Management: Help businesses enhance their online presence by managing their social media accounts, creating engaging content, and implementing marketing strategies.

4. Graphic Design Services: Provide graphic design solutions for businesses, including logo design, branding materials, marketing collateral, and website graphics.

5. Online Coaching and Consulting: Share your expertise in areas such as career coaching, wellness coaching, business consulting, or personal development through virtual coaching sessions and online courses.

6. E-commerce Store: Start an online store selling handmade crafts, vintage items, or niche

products catering to a specific audience or interest.

7. Event Planning and Coordination: Plan and execute weddings, parties, corporate events, and other special occasions for clients, handling everything from venue selection to vendor coordination.

8. Professional Organizing Services: Help individuals and businesses declutter and organize their spaces, offering services such as home organization, office organization, and downsizing assistance.

9. Dog Walking and Pet Sitting: Provide pet care services, including dog walking, pet sitting, and pet boarding, for busy pet owners in your local area.

10.Bookkeeping Services: Assist small businesses with their financial record-keeping, including bookkeeping, payroll processing, and tax preparation.

11. Legal Document Preparation and Notary Services: Offer assistance with legal document preparation, including contracts, leases, and agreements, as well as notary public services.

12. Property Management: Manage rental properties on behalf of landlords, handling tasks such as tenant screening, rent collection, maintenance coordination, and property inspections.

13. Tutoring and Educational Services: Provide tutoring services in subjects such as math, science, language arts, or test preparation for students of all ages.

14. Personal Chef and Meal Prep Services: Prepare customized meals and meal plans for individuals and families, catering to dietary preferences, restrictions, and health goals.

15. Handmade Crafts and Artisan Goods: Create and sell handmade crafts, artwork, jewelry, or

other artisan goods through online marketplaces, craft fairs, and pop-up shops.

16. Fitness Training and Wellness Coaching: Offer personal training, fitness classes, or wellness coaching services to help clients achieve their health and fitness goals.

17. Home Cleaning and Maid Services: Provide residential cleaning services, including regular cleaning, deep cleaning, and move-in/move-out cleaning, for busy homeowners and renters.

18. Digital Marketing Agency: Start a digital marketing agency offering services such as SEO, content marketing, email marketing, and PPC advertising to help businesses grow their online presence.

19. Recruiting and Staffing Agency: Help businesses find qualified candidates for job openings by providing recruiting, staffing, and placement services tailored to their needs.

20. Online Course Creation: Develop and sell online courses on topics such as business skills, personal development, hobby tutorials, or specialized knowledge to a global audience.

With creativity, determination, and a willingness to strive, female entrepreneurs can turn these business ideas into lucrative ventures that generate six figures and beyond, paving the way for financial independence and professional success.

Chapter 4: Building a Solid Foundation

Building a successful business requires a solid foundation. In this chapter, we'll explore the essential elements of laying that foundation, including setting clear goals and objectives, creating a comprehensive business plan, understanding legal considerations, and emphasizing the importance of good bookkeeping in your business.

Setting Clear Goals and Objectives

Setting clear goals and objectives is the first step in building a successful business. Goals provide direction and motivation, guiding your decisions and actions as you work towards achieving your vision. Here's how to set effective goals for your business:

Define Your Vision: Start by clarifying your long-term vision for your business. What do you hope to accomplish? What impact do you want to make in the world? Your vision should inspire and guide your goals.

Set SMART Goals: SMART goals are specific, measurable, achievable, relevant, and time-bound. Be specific about what you want to achieve, set measurable targets, ensure they are attainable, relevant to your vision, and set deadlines to keep yourself accountable.

Break Down Goals into Milestones: Break down your long-term goals into smaller, manageable milestones. This makes your goals more achievable and allows you to track your progress along the way.

Creating a Business Plan

A business plan is a roadmap that outlines your business goals, strategies, and financial projections. It serves as a guide for your business and helps you attract investors, secure funding, and make informed decisions. Here's what to include in your business plan:

Executive Summary: Summarize your business concept, mission, goals, and key highlights of your plan.

Business Description: Provide an overview of your business, including your products or services, target market, competitive analysis, and unique selling proposition.

Market Analysis: Conduct research on your industry, target market, and competitors. Identify market trends, customer needs, and opportunities for growth.

Marketing and Sales Strategy: Outline your marketing and sales strategies, including how you will promote your business, acquire customers, and generate revenue.

Operations and Management: Describe your business operations, organizational structure, and key personnel. Include information about your suppliers, partners, and vendors.

Financial Projections: Prepare financial forecasts, including income statements, cash flow projections, and balance sheets. This helps investors and lenders understand the financial viability of your business.

Legal Considerations for Entrepreneurs

Navigating the legal landscape is essential for protecting your business and ensuring compliance with relevant regulations. Here are some key legal considerations for entrepreneurs:

Business Structure: Choose the right legal structure for your business, such as a sole proprietorship, partnership, corporation, or limited liability company (LLC). Each structure has different tax implications, liability protections, and regulatory requirements.

Business Licenses and Permits: Research and obtain any necessary business licenses, permits, or certifications required to operate legally in your industry and location.

Intellectual Property Protection: Protect your intellectual property, including trademarks, copyrights, and patents. Consider filing for trademarks to safeguard your brand identity and prevent others from using similar names or logos.

Contracts and Agreements: Draft and review contracts and agreements carefully, including client contracts, vendor agreements, and employee contracts. Ensure that your legal documents are clear, comprehensive, and legally binding.

If you find yourself struggling to understand the legal obligations for your business, it's essential to seek professional guidance to ensure compliance and protect your interests. Hiring an Attorney, Freelance Paralegal, or Business Consultant can provide valuable assistance in navigating the complexities of business regulations and filling out necessary forms accurately. Legal obligations can expose your business to risks such as fines, penalties, lawsuits, or even regulatory shutdowns. A legal professional can help you identify and mitigate potential risks, protecting your business from legal consequences.

Importance of Good Bookkeeping

Good bookkeeping is essential for the financial health and success of your business. It involves recording, organizing, and tracking your business's financial transactions, expenses, and income. Here's why good bookkeeping is crucial:

Financial Management: Accurate bookkeeping allows you to track your business's financial performance, monitor cash flow, and make informed decisions about budgeting, spending, and investments.

Tax Compliance: Proper bookkeeping ensures that you maintain accurate records for tax purposes and comply with tax laws and regulations. This can help you avoid penalties, audits, and potential legal issues with tax authorities.

Business Planning: Detailed financial records provide valuable insights into your business's strengths, weaknesses, and opportunities for growth. This information is essential for creating realistic financial projections and strategic plans for your business.

Investor Confidence: If you plan to seek funding or investors for your business, organized and transparent financial records can instill confidence in potential investors. They want to see that you have a clear understanding of your finances and are capable of managing your business effectively.

Detailed Strategies for Effective Bookkeeping

1. Choose the Right Accounting System: Select an accounting system or software that meets your business needs and budget. Popular options include QuickBooks, Xero, and FreshBooks.

2. Maintain Separate Business Accounts: Keep your business finances separate from your personal finances by opening a business bank account and credit card. This makes it easier to track business expenses and income accurately.

3. Record Transactions Regularly: Make it a habit to record your business transactions regularly, whether it's daily, weekly, or monthly. This ensures that you have up-to-date financial records and reduces the risk of errors or oversights.

4. Organize Receipts and Invoices: Keep track of all your receipts, invoices, and financial documents in an organized manner. This makes it easier to reconcile accounts, prepare tax returns, and respond to any financial inquiries.

5. Reconcile Bank Statements: Reconcile your bank statements regularly to ensure that your accounting records match your actual bank transactions. This helps identify any discrepancies or errors that need to be corrected.

6. Monitor Cash Flow: Keep a close eye on your cash flow by tracking incoming and outgoing funds. This allows you to identify any cash flow issues early and take proactive measures to address them.

7. Stay Updated on Tax Laws: Stay informed about changes in tax laws and regulations that may affect your business. Consult with a tax professional if you have any questions or concerns about your tax obligations.

8. Seek Professional Help When Needed: If you're not confident in your bookkeeping skills or don't have the time to manage your finances, consider hiring a professional bookkeeper or accountant to assist you. This ensures that your financial records are accurate and compliant with regulations.

By implementing these strategies and prioritizing good bookkeeping practices, you can set your business up for long-term success and growth. Good bookkeeping not only helps you make better financial decisions but also provides peace of mind knowing that your business's finances are in order.

Conclusion

Building a solid foundation is essential for the success of your business. By setting clear goals and objectives, creating a comprehensive business plan, understanding legal considerations, and prioritizing good bookkeeping practices, you can lay the groundwork for a thriving and sustainable enterprise. Remember that building a business is a journey, and success takes time, dedication, and perseverance. Stay focused on your vision, adapt to challenges, and never stop learning and growing as an entrepreneur.

Chapter 5: The Power of Mindset and Confidence

In the journey of entrepreneurship, mindset and confidence play a pivotal role in determining success. This chapter delves into the significance of mindset and confidence, addressing the challenges of self-doubt and imposter syndrome, and providing strategies for cultivating a positive mindset and building confidence in yourself and your business.

Understanding the Power of Mindset and Confidence

Mindset refers to the attitudes, beliefs, and perspectives that shape our thoughts and behaviors. A positive mindset empowers us to overcome challenges, embrace opportunities, and persist in the face of adversity. Confidence, on the other hand, is the belief in oneself and one's abilities. It enables us to take risks, make bold decisions, and pursue our goals with determination.

Overcoming Self-Doubt and Imposter Syndrome

Self-doubt and imposter syndrome are common challenges that many entrepreneurs face. Self-doubt manifests as feelings of inadequacy or uncertainty about one's abilities, while imposter syndrome is the belief that one's success is undeserved or attributed to luck rather than skill. Overcoming these obstacles requires introspection and resilience.

Example: Sara Blakely, Founder of Spanx

Sara Blakely, the founder of Spanx, faced numerous rejections and setbacks before launching her successful shapewear brand. Despite encountering self-doubt and skepticism from others, Blakely persisted in pursuing her vision. She credits her resilience and positive mindset for overcoming obstacles and achieving success in a highly competitive industry.

Cultivating a Positive Mindset

Cultivating a positive mindset is essential for navigating the ups and downs of entrepreneurship. Here are some strategies for fostering positivity:

Practice Gratitude: Focus on what you're grateful for each day, even amidst challenges. Gratitude can shift your perspective and cultivate a sense of abundance.

Visualization: Visualize your goals and success regularly. Visualization can help reinforce positive beliefs and motivate you to take action towards your aspirations.

Positive Affirmations: Replace negative self-talk with positive affirmations. Affirmations can reframe your mindset and bolster your confidence in your abilities.

Building Confidence in Yourself and Your Business

Confidence is a key driver of success in entrepreneurship. Here's how to build confidence in yourself and your business:

Set Achievable Goals: Break down your goals into smaller, achievable tasks. Celebrate your successes along the way, no matter how small, to boost your confidence and momentum.

Write Down Your Goals: Writing down your goals can significantly boost self-confidence for several reasons:

1. Clarity and Focus: When you write down your goals, you clarify what you want to achieve and give yourself a clear target to aim for. This clarity and focus reduce uncertainty and indecision, making it easier to take action towards your goals with confidence.

2. Concrete Commitment: Putting your goals on paper is a concrete commitment to yourself. It signifies your dedication and determination to achieve those goals, which in turn bolsters your confidence in your ability to follow through and succeed.

3. Trackable Progress: By writing down your goals, you create a tangible record of your aspirations. As you make progress towards your goals and check off milestones, you can see how far you've come, which boosts confidence and motivation.

4. Accountability: When your goals are written down, you hold yourself accountable for achieving them. This accountability instills a sense of responsibility and ownership, empowering you to take proactive steps towards your goals with confidence.

5. Visual Reinforcement: Seeing your goals written down reinforces them in your mind and serves as a constant reminder of what you're

working towards. This visual reinforcement helps keep your goals top of mind and strengthens your belief in their attainability.

6. Problem-Solving and Adaptation: When you encounter obstacles or setbacks on your journey, having your goals written down allows you to evaluate your progress objectively and adapt your approach as needed. This problem-solving mindset reinforces your confidence in your ability to overcome challenges and find solutions.

7. Celebrating Achievements: Writing down your goals allows you to celebrate your achievements along the way, no matter how small. Celebrating wins reinforces your confidence and motivates you to continue pushing towards your goals.

8. Embrace Failure as a Learning Opportunity: View failure as a natural part of the entrepreneurial journey rather than a reflection of your worth. Learn from your mistakes, adapt, and keep moving forward.

9. Surround Yourself with Supportive People**: Surround yourself with a supportive network of mentors, peers, and friends who believe in you and your vision. Their encouragement and guidance can bolster your confidence during challenging times.

Example: Oprah Winfrey

Oprah Winfrey, media mogul and philanthropist, is a prime example of confidence and resilience in the face of adversity. Oprah Winfrey's confidence and resilience in the face of adversity played a significant role in her journey to success. Here are three examples of how her mindset propelled her forward:

1. Overcoming Childhood Adversity: Oprah Winfrey faced numerous challenges and adversity during her childhood, including poverty, abuse, and instability. Despite these obstacles, she remained resilient and determined to create a better future for herself. Oprah's confidence in her own abilities allowed her to

see beyond her circumstances and believe in her potential for success. Rather than being defined by her past, she used her experiences as fuel to drive her forward, ultimately becoming one of the most influential media moguls in the world.

2. Navigating Career Setbacks: Throughout her career, Oprah encountered setbacks and challenges that tested her resilience. Early in her broadcasting career, she faced criticism and discrimination as a black woman in a predominantly white industry. Despite these obstacles, Oprah refused to be discouraged or sidelined. Her unwavering confidence in her talent and vision propelled her to persevere, and she eventually became the host of her own talk show, "The Oprah Winfrey Show," which became one of the highest-rated television programs of its kind.

3. Championing Personal Growth and Empowerment: Oprah Winfrey's confidence and resilience are evident in her commitment to personal growth and empowerment. Throughout her career, she has fearlessly tackled taboo topics, challenged societal norms, and advocated

for marginalized communities. Oprah's confidence in her voice and platform allowed her to use her influence for positive change, inspiring millions of people around the world to live their best lives. Through her multimedia empire, she continues to empower others to overcome adversity, pursue their dreams, and make a difference in the world.

Despite facing numerous obstacles throughout her career, including poverty, abuse, and discrimination, Winfrey persevered and became one of the most influential figures in the world. She attributes her success to her unwavering belief in herself and her ability to overcome challenges with grace and determination.

Personal Reflection and Application

Take some time to reflect on your own mindset and confidence levels. Identify any negative beliefs or self-limiting beliefs that may be holding you back. Challenge these beliefs and replace them with positive affirmations and empowering thoughts. Consider how you can incorporate the strategies mentioned in this chapter into your daily routine to cultivate a positive mindset and build confidence in yourself and your business.

Remember that mindset and confidence are not fixed traits but skills that can be developed and strengthened over time. By fostering a positive mindset and belief in yourself, you can overcome obstacles, seize opportunities, and achieve success in your entrepreneurial journey.

Chapter 6: Strategic Branding and Marketing

Effective branding and marketing are essential for building a successful business. In this chapter, we will explore the importance of crafting a strong brand identity, developing a comprehensive marketing strategy, and leveraging social media and online platforms to reach your target audience.

Crafting Your Brand Identity

Your brand identity is the essence of your business - it encompasses your values, personality, and the promise you make to your customers. Here's how to craft a compelling brand identity:

1. Define Your Brand Values: Start by identifying the core values that define your business. What do you stand for? What sets you apart from competitors? Your brand values should resonate with your target audience and guide your brand's actions and decisions.

2. Create a Unique Brand Voice and Tone: Your brand voice and tone reflect the personality of your business. Whether it's playful and casual or professional and authoritative, consistency is key. Your brand voice should be reflected in all communication channels, from social media posts to customer service interactions.

3. Design Your Visual Brand Elements: Visual elements such as your logo, color palette, and typography are crucial for conveying your brand identity visually. Invest in professional design that reflects your brand personality and resonates with your target audience.

4. Craft Your Brand Story: A compelling brand story helps humanize your brand and connect with your audience on an emotional level. Share

your journey, values, and mission in a way that resonates with your audience and inspires loyalty.

Developing a Marketing Strategy

A well-defined marketing strategy helps you reach your target audience, build brand awareness, and drive sales. Here's how to develop an effective marketing strategy:

1. Identify Your Target Audience: Understand who your ideal customers are, what their needs and pain points are, and where they hang out online and offline. This information will inform your marketing efforts and help you tailor your messaging to resonate with your audience.

2. Set Clear Marketing Objectives: Define specific, measurable marketing objectives that align with your overall business goals. Whether it's increasing brand awareness, generating leads, or driving sales, your objectives should be realistic and achievable.

3. Choose the Right Marketing Channels: Select marketing channels that are most relevant to your target audience and align with your brand identity. This may include a mix of digital channels such as social media, email marketing, content marketing, as well as traditional channels like print ads or events.

4. Create Compelling Content: Content is the cornerstone of any marketing strategy. Develop high-quality, engaging content that provides value to your audience and showcases your expertise. This could include blog posts, videos, infographics, podcasts, or user-generated content.

Utilizing Social Media and Online Platforms

Social media and online platforms offer powerful tools for reaching and engaging with your target audience. Here's how to leverage them effectively:

1. Choose the Right Platforms: Identify which social media platforms your target audience uses most frequently and focus your efforts there. Whether it's Facebook, Instagram, Twitter, LinkedIn, or TikTok, each platform has its own unique audience and features.

2. Create Engaging Content: Develop a content strategy tailored to each platform and audience. Share a mix of informative, entertaining, and promotional content to keep your audience engaged and interested in your brand.

3. Engage with Your Audience: Social media is a two-way conversation. Respond promptly to comments, messages, and mentions, and actively engage with your audience through likes, shares, and comments. Building genuine connections with your audience fosters trust and loyalty.

4. Monitor and Measure Performance: Track key metrics such as engagement, reach, and conversions to assess the effectiveness of your social media and online marketing efforts. Use analytics tools to gain insights into what's working well and where you can improve.

By crafting a strong brand identity, developing a comprehensive marketing strategy, and leveraging social media and online platforms effectively, you can increase brand awareness, engage with your target audience, and drive growth for your business.

Chapter 7: Financial Management and Wealth Building

Financial management is the backbone of a successful business. In this chapter, we'll explore the importance of budgeting and financial planning, managing cash flow and expenses, and investing for long-term success.

Budgeting and Financial Planning

Budgeting and financial planning are essential for setting financial goals, allocating resources effectively, and ensuring the financial health of your business. Here's how to approach budgeting and financial planning:

1. Set Clear Financial Goals: Define your short-term and long-term financial goals, such as

increasing revenue, reducing expenses, or saving for expansion. Your goals should be specific, measurable, achievable, relevant, and time-bound (SMART).

2. Create a Budget: Develop a comprehensive budget that outlines your projected income and expenses for a specific period, typically monthly or annually. Allocate funds to different categories, including operating expenses, marketing, payroll, and taxes.

3. Track and Monitor Expenses: Regularly monitor your expenses to ensure they align with your budget and financial goals. Identify areas where you can reduce costs or reallocate resources to maximize efficiency and profitability.

4. Plan for Contingencies: Anticipate unexpected expenses or fluctuations in revenue by building a contingency fund. Having a financial safety net in place allows you to weather unforeseen challenges without jeopardizing your business's stability.

Managing Cash Flow and Expenses

Cash flow management is crucial for maintaining liquidity and ensuring your business's financial stability. Here's how to effectively manage cash flow and expenses:

1. Monitor Cash Flow: Track your incoming and outgoing cash flow regularly to identify patterns and trends. Use cash flow projections to anticipate future cash needs and plan accordingly.

2. Manage Accounts Receivable and Payable: Implement strategies to optimize accounts receivable and payable processes. Invoice customers promptly, follow up on overdue payments, and negotiate favorable payment terms with suppliers to maintain positive cash flow.

3. Control Operating Expenses: Review your operating expenses regularly and look for opportunities to reduce costs without sacrificing

quality or efficiency. Negotiate contracts with vendors, explore alternative suppliers, and streamline internal processes to minimize expenses.

4. Maintain Adequate Working Capital: Ensure you have sufficient working capital to cover day-to-day operational expenses and unexpected cash flow gaps. Consider options such as lines of credit or business loans to bridge short-term funding needs.

Investing for Long-Term Success

Investing wisely is key to achieving long-term financial success and building wealth for your business. Here's how to approach investing for long-term growth:

1. Diversify Your Investments: Spread your investments across different asset classes, industries, and geographic regions to reduce risk and maximize returns. Diversification helps

safeguard your portfolio against market volatility and economic downturns.

2. Focus on Growth Opportunities: Identify investment opportunities that have the potential for long-term growth and profitability. This may include expanding into new markets, investing in research and development, or acquiring complementary businesses.

3. Consider Risk Management: Assess the risks associated with each investment opportunity and develop strategies to mitigate potential downsides. Conduct thorough due diligence, seek expert advice, and diversify your investments to minimize risk exposure.

4. Monitor and Review Investments: Regularly review your investment portfolio and performance to ensure it aligns with your financial goals and risk tolerance. Adjust your investment strategy as needed based on changing market conditions and business objectives.

By implementing effective budgeting and financial planning, managing cash flow and expenses, and investing for long-term success, you can build a solid financial foundation for your business and create opportunities for sustainable growth and prosperity.

Chapter 8: Scaling Your Business for Six Figures

Scaling your business for six figures requires strategic planning, leveraging opportunities, and building a strong foundation for growth. In this chapter, we'll explore scaling strategies, growth opportunities, leveraging technology and automation, and building a strong team and network.

Scaling Strategies and Growth Opportunities

Scaling a business involves expanding its operations to accommodate increased demand while maintaining or improving profitability. Here are some scaling strategies and growth opportunities to consider:

Market Expansion: Identify new markets or customer segments to target with your products or services. This may involve geographic expansion, tapping into niche markets, or diversifying your offerings to appeal to a broader audience. It involves identifying and tapping into untapped opportunities to increase sales, revenue, and market share. Here's a detailed explanation of market expansion:

1. Geographic Expansion: One of the most common forms of market expansion is geographic expansion, which involves entering new geographic regions or territories to reach a broader audience. This could include expanding locally, regionally, nationally, or internationally, depending on the business's growth ambitions and market potential.

Example: You're the owner of a boutique in a single city. You decide that you want to open new storefronts in neighboring towns and cities to reach customers outside its current market. By expanding geographically, you attract new customers who may not have easy access to your products.

2. Demographic Diversification: Another approach to market expansion is demographic diversification, which involves targeting new customer segments based on demographic characteristics such as age, gender, income level, or lifestyle preferences. This allows businesses to appeal to a wider range of customers with different needs and preferences.

Example: You own a subscription meal delivery service that initially targets busy professionals, but you decide to expand your customer base by offering specialized meal plans for families, seniors, and athletes. By diversifying the offerings, your company can attract a broader audience and increase market penetration. *

3. Product/Service Differentiation: Market expansion can also involve diversifying or expanding the range of products or services offered to meet the needs of new customer segments or markets. This could include introducing new product lines, variations, or complementary services that appeal to different customer preferences or market segments.

Example: You're the owner of a software company that specializes in project management tools and you decide to expand the product offerings by introducing collaboration and communication tools tailored for small businesses. By diversifying the product portfolio, your company can appeal to a broader range of customers and industries. *

4. Online Market Expansion: In today's digital age, market expansion often involves leveraging online channels and platforms to reach new customers and markets. This could include selling products or services through e-commerce websites, online marketplaces, or digital advertising campaigns targeted at specific demographic or geographic segments.

Example: You're a handmade jewelry artisan who sells your creations at local craft fairs and you decide to expand your market reach by opening an online store on a popular e-commerce platform. By reaching customers beyond your local area, you can significantly increase sales and exposure for your products.

5. Strategic Partnerships and Alliances: Another approach to market expansion is through strategic partnerships and alliances with other businesses or organizations. By collaborating with complementary businesses, sharing resources, or entering into joint ventures, companies can access new markets, distribution channels, and customer bases.

Example: You're the owner of a cleaning company. Your company does turnover cleans for short-term rentals. You partner with a linen company. By leveraging each other's customer base and brand loyalty, both businesses can expand their reach and attract new customers.

6. Franchising or Licensing: Expand your business through franchising or licensing arrangements, allowing others to replicate your business model and brand in different locations or markets. This can accelerate growth while minimizing the need for significant capital investment.

Example: A successful restaurant concept franchises its brand and operations to entrepreneurs interested in opening their own locations, expanding its footprint and revenue streams.

Leveraging Technology and Automation

Technology and automation play a crucial role in scaling your business efficiently and effectively. Here's how to leverage technology and automation to streamline operations and drive growth:

1. Implement Cloud-Based Solutions: Adopt cloud-based software and tools for managing various aspects of your business, such as accounting, project management, customer relationship management (CRM), and collaboration. Cloud-based solutions offer scalability, flexibility, and accessibility, allowing you to manage your business from anywhere.

Example: You're an e-commerce retailer that invests in a cloud-based inventory management system that automatically adjusts inventory levels, tracks sales trends, and generates purchase orders as needed, enabling seamless scalability.

2. Automate Repetitive Tasks: Identify repetitive or manual tasks that can be automated to free up time and resources for more strategic activities. This may include email marketing automation, customer service chatbots, or workflow automation tools.

Example: A subscription box service automates order processing, shipping notifications, and customer feedback surveys, allowing the team to focus on curating new products and improving the customer experience.

3. Utilize Data Analytics: Leverage data analytics and business intelligence tools to gain insights into customer behavior, market trends, and operational efficiency. Use data-driven decision-

making to optimize processes, identify growth opportunities, and drive strategic initiatives.

Example: A SaaS company analyzes user engagement metrics and customer feedback to identify key features for product development and prioritize roadmap initiatives, resulting in higher customer satisfaction and retention.

4. Artificial Intelligence: Artificial Intelligence (AI) has emerged as a powerful tool for leveraging technology and automation across various industries. By harnessing the capabilities of AI, businesses can streamline processes, improve efficiency, and unlock new opportunities for innovation.

Example: You own a multinational e-commerce company that receives thousands of customer inquiries each day. By implementing an AI-powered chatbot on your website, your company can automate responses to common questions about product availability, shipping times, return policies, and order status. The chatbot uses AI algorithms to analyze customer queries, identify relevant information from a knowledge base, and provide accurate and personalized responses in real-time. This not only improves the overall customer experience by offering instant support but also reduces the workload on human agents, allowing them to handle more complex issues and provide higher-value assistance when needed.

Building a Strong Team and Network

A strong team and network are essential for supporting business growth and scalability. Here's how to build and leverage your team and network effectively:

1. Hire and Develop Top Talent: Recruit skilled and motivated employees who align with your company culture and values. Invest in ongoing training and development programs to nurture talent, foster growth, and retain top performers.

   Example: Your tech startup company offers professional development opportunities, mentorship programs, and competitive benefits to attract and retain top engineering talent, fueling innovation and product development.

2. Subcontracting: This helps small businesses to access specialized expertise and talent that they may not have in-house, helping to strengthen their team without the need for full-time hires. By outsourcing specific tasks or projects to experienced professionals or agencies, small businesses can fill skill gaps, increase efficiency, and focus on core activities.

Example: Your small marketing agency may subcontract graphic design work to a freelance designer, enabling them to offer high-quality design services to clients without the overhead costs of hiring a full-time designer.

3. Part-Time Intern: Taking on a part-time intern in a small business provides an opportunity to mentor and develop young talent while gaining additional support for projects and tasks. Interns bring fresh perspectives, enthusiasm, and a

willingness to learn, contributing new ideas and energy to the team dynamic.

Example: You're a family-owned bakery that hired a part-time intern to assist with baking, customer service, and social media marketing, allowing your business to expand its operations and serve more customers while providing valuable hands-on training to the intern.

4. Delegate and Empower: Delegate tasks and responsibilities to capable team members to empower them to take ownership and contribute to the company's success. Trust your team to make decisions and provide support and guidance as needed.

Example: You delegate administrative tasks to a virtual assistant, allowing them to focus on strategic initiatives and business development activities, leading to increased productivity and growth.

5. Build a Supportive Network: Cultivate relationships with mentors, advisors, industry peers, and potential collaborators who can provide guidance, support, and opportunities for growth. Actively participate in networking events, industry conferences, and online communities to expand your network.

Example: You're an aspiring entrepreneur and you join the chamber of commerce within your area. You attend the chamber's business networking events and conferences to connect with seasoned professionals, seek advice, and explore partnership opportunities, expanding your network and business opportunities.

By implementing effective scaling strategies, leveraging technology and automation, and building a strong team and network, you can position your business for sustainable growth and success. Stay agile, adaptable, and focused on your long-term vision as you navigate the challenges and opportunities of scaling your business for six figures.

Chapter 9: Overcoming Obstacles and Resilience

Embarking on the journey of entrepreneurship as a woman comes with its own set of challenges, including facing setbacks and failures along the way. In this chapter, we'll explore strategies for overcoming the fear of failure, building resilience, and persevering through obstacles to achieve success.

1. Understanding Setbacks and Failures

Setbacks and failures are an inevitable part of the entrepreneurial journey. They can come in many forms, such as financial losses, product launches that don't meet expectations, or deals that fall through. It's essential to recognize that setbacks are not a reflection of your worth or abilities but rather opportunities for growth and learning.

2. Overcoming the Fear of Failure

Fear of failure can be paralyzing and prevent aspiring female entrepreneurs from taking risks and pursuing their dreams. To overcome this fear:

- Reframe Failure as Feedback: Instead of viewing failure as a final verdict, see it as valuable feedback that can inform your next steps and help you improve.

- Focus on Growth Mindset: Adopt a growth mindset, believing that your abilities and intelligence can be developed through effort and perseverance. Embrace challenges as opportunities to learn and grow.

3. Building Resilience and Perseverance

Resilience is the ability to bounce back from setbacks and adversity, while perseverance is the determination to keep moving forward despite obstacles. Here's how to build resilience and perseverance as a female entrepreneur:

- Seek Support and Mentorship: Surround yourself with a supportive network of mentors, peers, and advisors who can provide guidance, encouragement, and perspective during challenging times.

- Learn from Failure: Instead of dwelling on failure, extract valuable lessons from the experience. Reflect on what went wrong, what you could have done differently, and how you can apply these insights to future endeavors.

- Stay Flexible and Adapt* In the face of setbacks, be willing to pivot and adapt your strategies or goals as needed. Flexibility and adaptability are key traits of successful entrepreneurs who can navigate changing circumstances and market conditions.

4. Example: Cathy Hughes, Founder of Urban One

Cathy Hughes, the founder of Urban One (formerly Radio One), is a prime example of resilience and perseverance in the face of adversity. Despite facing numerous setbacks and obstacles throughout her career, including bankruptcy, rejection, and racial discrimination, Hughes remained undeterred in her pursuit of success.

When her first radio station acquisition deal fell through, Hughes didn't give up. Instead, she persevered, eventually securing financing and launching Radio One, which grew into the largest African American-owned broadcasting company in the United States. Through resilience, determination, and unwavering belief in her vision, Hughes overcame adversity and built a media empire that continues to thrive today.

Setbacks and failures are inevitable in the entrepreneurial journey, but they can also serve as catalysts for growth and success. By overcoming the fear of failure, building resilience, and persevering through obstacles, female entrepreneurs can overcome challenges, achieve their goals, and make a lasting impact in the business world.

Chapter 10: Nurturing Work-Life Harmony

Achieving a harmonious balance between work and life is essential for sustaining long-term success and well-being as a female entrepreneur. In this chapter, we'll delve into strategies for prioritizing self-care, managing family and business responsibilities, and nurturing overall well-being to achieve a fulfilling work-life balance.

1. Prioritizing Self-Care and Wellbeing

Make self-care a non-negotiable priority in your daily routine. Schedule regular breaks, exercise, and relaxation time to recharge and rejuvenate your mind and body. Practice mindfulness, meditation, or other stress-reducing techniques to maintain mental clarity and emotional resilience amidst the demands of entrepreneurship.

2. Setting Boundaries and Managing Time Effectively

Establish clear boundaries between work and personal life to prevent burnout and maintain balance. Set specific work hours, designate dedicated workspace, and communicate your availability and expectations to clients, colleagues, and family members. Utilize time management tools and techniques to prioritize tasks, delegate responsibilities, and optimize productivity.

3. Leveraging Technology and Outsourcing

Leverage technology and outsourcing solutions to streamline workflows, automate repetitive tasks, and free up time for more meaningful activities. Use project management software, virtual assistants, and other digital tools to enhance efficiency and effectiveness in managing both business and personal responsibilities.

4. Cultivating Supportive Relationships

Nurture supportive relationships with friends, family, and mentors who understand and respect your entrepreneurial journey. Lean on your support network for encouragement, advice, and emotional support during challenging times. Communicate openly with loved ones about your business commitments and needs, fostering understanding and cooperation in balancing family and business responsibilities.

5. Practicing Flexibility and Adaptability

Embrace flexibility and adaptability as essential skills for navigating the unpredictable nature of entrepreneurship and life. Be willing to adjust your schedule, priorities, and expectations as needed to accommodate changing circumstances and unexpected challenges. Maintain a growth mindset, viewing setbacks and obstacles as opportunities for learning and growth rather than roadblocks.

By prioritizing self-care and wellbeing, setting boundaries, leveraging technology and outsourcing, cultivating supportive relationships, and practicing flexibility and adaptability, you can achieve a harmonious work-life balance as a female entrepreneur. Remember that finding balance is an ongoing journey, and it's okay to reassess and recalibrate your approach as you evolve personally and professionally. Ultimately, nurturing work-life harmony is key to sustaining fulfillment, happiness, and success in both your business and personal endeavors.

Chapter 11: Paying It Forward: Empowering Other Women

As female entrepreneurs, we have a unique opportunity and responsibility to uplift and empower other women on their entrepreneurial journey. In this chapter, we'll explore the power of mentorship and support networks, the importance of giving back to the community, and how each of us can be a catalyst for positive change in the lives of others.

1. Mentorship and Support Networks

Recognize the transformative impact of mentorship and support networks in fostering the growth and success of aspiring female entrepreneurs. Share your knowledge, insights, and experiences with others, serving as a mentor or role model for women who are navigating the challenges of entrepreneurship. Seek out mentorship opportunities for yourself, connecting with experienced professionals who can offer guidance, advice, and support as you continue to grow and evolve in your own entrepreneurial journey.

2. Creating a Culture of Collaboration

Foster a culture of collaboration and community among women in business, recognizing that we are stronger together than we are apart. Collaborate with other female entrepreneurs, share resources, and support each other's ventures through partnerships, referrals, and joint ventures. Celebrate the achievements and successes of other women in business, lifting each other up and amplifying each other's voices in a spirit of solidarity and sisterhood.

3. Giving Back to the Community

Acknowledge the importance of giving back to the community as a way of paying forward the support and opportunities you've received on your entrepreneurial journey. Find ways to contribute to causes and organizations that align with your values and passions, whether through volunteering your time, donating resources, or using your platform to raise awareness and advocate for change. By giving back to the community, you not only make a positive impact on the lives of others but also cultivate a sense of purpose and fulfillment in your own life and work.

4. Being a Catalyst for Change

Embrace your role as a catalyst for change and progress in your industry, your community, and the world at large. Use your voice, influence, and platform to champion causes that matter to you, whether it's advocating for gender equality, diversity and inclusion, environmental sustainability, or social justice. Take action to address systemic barriers and inequities, working towards a more inclusive and equitable future where all women have the opportunity to thrive and succeed.

5. Inspiring the Next Generation

Inspire and empower the next generation of female entrepreneurs by sharing your story, your struggles, and your successes with young women and girls. Serve as a mentor, role model, and advocate for future generations, helping to cultivate a pipeline of empowered, ambitious, and resilient female leaders who will continue to drive positive change and innovation in the years to come.

By paying it forward, empowering other women, fostering mentorship and support networks, giving back to the community, and being a catalyst for change, you can make a meaningful and lasting impact on the lives of others and create a more inclusive, equitable, and empowering world for women in entrepreneurship. Remember that the ripple effects of your actions and contributions have the power to inspire and uplift countless others, creating a legacy of empowerment and opportunity that transcends generations.

Conclusion

In "SHEO: A Guide to Female Entrepreneurship and Financial Freedom," we have embarked on a journey to explore the transformative power of women in the entrepreneurial landscape. Throughout these pages, we have witnessed the indomitable spirit, resilience, and creativity that define female entrepreneurs worldwide. From overcoming barriers to seizing opportunities, women have demonstrated their capacity to drive innovation, foster economic growth, and effect positive change in their communities.

However, our exploration does not end here; it merely marks the beginning of a new chapter in the ongoing quest for gender equality and empowerment. As we conclude our journey, let us reaffirm our commitment to creating an environment where every woman can pursue her entrepreneurial dreams and achieve financial independence.

Let us dismantle the systemic barriers that hinder women's progress and embrace diversity and inclusivity as catalysts for innovation and prosperity. Let us amplify the voices of female entrepreneurs, celebrate their successes, and learn from their experiences.

As we look towards the future, let us envision a world where SHEOs (She Entrepreneurs) thrive, not just for the sake of economic advancement, but as agents of social change, champions of equality, and architects of a more equitable and sustainable future for all.

In the end, "SHEO" is not just a guidebook; it is a manifesto—a call to action for individuals, communities, and policymakers to join hands in creating a world where every woman can unleash her full potential and soar to new heights of success and fulfillment.

Together, let us pave the way towards a future where female entrepreneurship flourishes, and financial freedom knows no gender.

Acknowledgements

I would like to express my deepest gratitude to everyone who has contributed to the creation of this book. Special thanks to Latasha and Sumairah for their invaluable support and encouragement throughout this journey. This book would not have been possible without you.

Katharine Wolf and the Odettians, thank you for listening to my story. It has motivated me to continue to inspire women as you have and continue to do.

Zoe, Zanai, Paul Fyffe, Reese, Sandra Paredes, Tanisha S, Simone W, Natasha Mclean, Winston, Rondell A, Nicole, Marilyn, Paul Campbell, Chante Campbell, Renee, Nikiya H, Amanda Appi, Taylor K, Jamie, and Vanessa Perez. Your constant support and listening ears keep me grounded.

Jemp Pena and the Relay Task team, thank you for being the backbone of A & B Personnel Services, LLC.

Biography

Ashona Fyffe is a mother, entrepreneur, and aspiring Business Immigration Attorney. Raised in the vibrant neighborhood of Flatbush, Brooklyn, New York, she embodies the spirit of determination and resilience that characterizes her community. As the daughter of Jamaican immigrants, she is deeply rooted in her cultural heritage and carries the legacy of her family's journey to America.

Growing up in a household that instilled the values of hard work and perseverance, Ashona Fyffe recognized early on the transformative power of education and entrepreneurship. With a burning desire to make a difference in the lives of others, she embarked on a journey of academic and professional pursuits. She graduated from Hunter College with a B.S. in Accounting.

Fueled by her personal experiences and a desire to make a difference, Ashona Fyffe became an advocate for women. With a vision to empower women entrepreneurs like herself, she founded A & B Personnel Services LLC. Her company provides legal document preparation and bookkeeping services to female-owned businesses.

As the author of "SHEO: A Guide to Female Entrepreneurship and Financial Freedom," Ashona Fyffe shares her expertise, insights, and personal journey to inspire and empower women to pursue their entrepreneurial dreams. Through her book, she aims to provide practical guidance and support to aspiring female entrepreneurs, while also igniting a conversation about the importance of female empowerment and the transformative potential of entrepreneurship.

In Ashona Fyffe, we see not just an author or entrepreneur, but a trailblazer—a champion for change, equality, and the realization of dreams. Her story serves as an inspiration for women everywhere, reminding us that with perseverance, passion, and determination, anything is possible.

Resources for female-owned businesses

1. **Grants:**

   - Amber Grant: Offers a $10,000 grant each month to a female entrepreneur.

   - The Cartier Women's Initiative: Provides funding, mentoring, and networking opportunities for female entrepreneurs.

   - Eileen Fisher Women-Owned Business Grant Program: Offers grants to women-owned businesses that are beyond the startup phase and ready to expand.

   - FedEx Small Business Grant Contest: Provides grants, prizes, and business support to small businesses, including those owned by women.

   - Women's Business Enterprise National Council (WBENC) Grants: WBENC often partners with corporations to offer grants and opportunities for women-owned businesses.

2. **Small Business Administration (SBA):**

   - SBA Women's Business Centers: Offers counseling, training, and networking opportunities specifically tailored to female entrepreneurs.

   - SBA Loans and Grants: The SBA provides various loan programs and grants that are accessible to women-owned businesses.

   - SBA Office of Women's Business Ownership: Offers resources, training, and support for women entrepreneurs, including access to government contracting opportunities.

3. **SCORE (Service Corps of Retired Executives):**

   - SCORE Women's Business Initiative: Provides mentoring, workshops, and resources tailored to female entrepreneurs.

   - SCORE Webinars and Workshops: Offers free online webinars and in-person workshops covering various aspects of business ownership, including those relevant to women-owned businesses.

4. **National Association of Women Business Owners (NAWBO):**

   - NAWBO Institute for Entrepreneurial Development: Offers programs, resources, and networking opportunities to help women business owners grow and scale their businesses.

   - NAWBO Mentoring Program: Matches experienced women entrepreneurs with mentees seeking guidance and support in their business endeavors.

5. **Women's Business Development Centers (WBDC):**

   - WBDC Business Development Programs: Provides training, counseling, and access to capital for women entrepreneurs.

   - WBDC Women's Business Enterprise Certification: Helps women-owned businesses obtain certification, which can open doors to contracting opportunities with government and corporate entities.

6. **Women's Entrepreneurship Day Organization (WEDO):**

   - WEDO Resources and Events: Offers resources, events, and initiatives aimed at empowering and supporting women entrepreneurs globally.

7. **Local Chambers of Commerce and Economic Development Organizations:**

   - Many local chambers of commerce and economic development organizations offer programs, grants, and resources specifically tailored to women-owned businesses. It's worth exploring what's available in your area.

These resources can provide valuable support, guidance, and opportunities for female entrepreneurs at various stages of their business journey.

Women Owned Business Referrals

1. A & B Personnel Services LLC- abpersonnelservices.com/legaldocumentpreparation

assistant@abpersonnelservices.com (Legal Document Preparation, Bookkeeping, Business Consulting, Business Process Outsourcing)

2. Accurate Payroll & Bookkeeping Services LLC- accuratepayrollbookkeeping.com

info@accuratepayrollbookkeeping.com (Payroll & Bookkeeping)

3. Timeless Remodels- novaemoney.com/chanldaniels/home

chanel.daniels@timelessremodels.com (Finance Solutions)

4. Immaculate Investigations LLC- southcarolinadetectiveagency.com

intake@immaculatepi.com (Private Investigations & Background Screenings)

5. Odetta, Inc.- Odetta.ai

katharine@odetta.ai (Technology, Information, and Internet)

6. Rubees Cleaners & Staffing- rubeescleaners23@gmail.com (Cleaning & Staffing)

7. Juice Plus- Daphne.juiceplus.com (Health Coach)

daphnejuiceplus@gmail.com

8. Posh Pets by Sumeshe - poshpetsbysumeshe@gmail.com (Exotic Cats & Dogs)

9. VersaLingo Interpreters- vaneli.perez@gmail.com (Interpreter)

10. Kimberly Fowler- Kimberly.fowler@exprealty.com (Realtor-South Carolina)

11. Pick A Party- pickapartymb.com (Event Planning & Balloon Décor)

843-580-1611

12. Rise N Shine Linen Services- rnslinenservices.com

rnslinenservices@gmail.com (Linen Laundering)

13. Indigenous HER Beauty Hair Care- natawahcorporation@gmail.com (Hair Care)

14. JustThinkAboutIt- justthinkaboutit@gmail.com (Nonprofit)

15. Imani's Safehouse Inc.- jenn.f@imanissafehouse.org (Nonprofit)

16. Snack Angel Vending Machine Placement Services LLC- snackangelvending@gmail.com (Vending Machine Placement)

17. Dakota's Document Preparation, LLC- anjeliai006@yahoo.com (Legal Document Preparation)

www.ingramcontent.com/pod-product-compliance
Lightning Source LLC
Chambersburg PA
CBHW031441210526
45464CB00005B/2292